THE VIKINGS

Clare Hibbert

First published in 2015 by Wayland
Copyright © Wayland 2014

Dewey Number: 941'.01-dc23
ISBN: 978-0-7502-9418-8
eBook ISBN: 978-0-7502-8550-6

10 9 8 7 6 5 4 3 2 1

The History Detective Investigates series:

Produced for Wayland by
White-Thomson Publishing Ltd
www.wtpub.co.uk
+44 (0)843 208 7460

Editor: Clare Hibbert
Designer: Alix Wood
Cover design concept: Lisa Peacock
Consultant: Philip Parker
Proofreader: Lucy Ross

Printed in Malaysia

Wayland
An imprint of Hachette Children's Group
Part of Hodder & Stoughton
Carmelite House, 50 Victoria Embankment
London EC4Y 0DZ

Wayland is a division of Hachette Children's Books,
an Hachette UK company

Picture Acknowledgments: Stefan Chabluk:
6b **Corbis:** 14 (Ted Spiegel); **Dreamstime:** 2
(Santiago Rodríguez Fontoba), 7b (Colin Young), 8
(Pablo Mendez Rodriguez), 12 (Nightman1965), 13t
(Mikelane45), 13b (Cerealphotos), 16 (Algol), 19t (Olga
Lipatova), 26r (Anders Rikard); **Shutterstock:** folios
(OlegDoroshin), 5t (Ivanukh), 11b (jps), 18 (Eugene
Sergeev); **TopFoto:** cover b (Jonathan Mitchell), 5b
(CM Dixon/Heritage Images), 10 (Granger Collection),
19b (Ancient Art & Architecture Collection);
Werner Forman Archive: 4 (Upplandsmuseet,
Uppsala), 6, 11t, 22, 23l, 23r, 25r, 27 and 29b (Statens
Historiska Museum, Stockholm), 15l (City & County
Museum, Lincoln), 17b (Bergen Maritime Museum),
20 (Universitetets Oldsaksamling, Oslo), 21b (Stofnun
Arna Magnussonar), 26l; **Wikimedia:** cover t (Berig/
The Man in Question), 1 (dalbera), 7c (Olaus Magnus),
9t (Erik), 9b (Holger.Ellgaard), 15b (Annie Dalbéra), 17t
(Dalbera), 21t (Nachosan), 24 (Museum
of Cultural History, Oslo University),
25t, Torvindus, 25bl (Frank
Axelsson), 28 (Matthew Paris), 29t
(Helen Simonsson).

Above: A statue of Leif Ericsson, who founded a
Viking colony in North America around 1000 CE.

Previous page: A carving of a Viking decorating a cart
in a **ship burial** found at Oseberg, Norway.

Cover top: Part of a stone that shows the god Odin
using his spear to push someone into a burial mound.

Cover bottom: Remains of a Viking **longhouse** at
Jarlshof, on Shetland, Scotland. The site was home
to **Norse** settlers from the 800s to the 1300s.

CONTENTS

Words in **bold** can be found in the glossary on page 30.

 The history detective Sherlock Bones will help you to find clues and collect evidence about the Vikings. Wherever you see one of Sherlock's paw-prints, you will find a mystery to solve. The answers are on page 31.

WHO WERE THE VIKINGS?

The Vikings were people who lived in Scandinavia between about 750 and 1100 CE. They were farmers and craftworkers. Some took to the seas as merchants, while others became raiders who terrorized other lands and were said to have gone 'a Viking'. Some were explorers and settlers. The Vikings had complex beliefs and their own writing system that used symbols called runes.

DETECTIVE WORK

Find out who the Vikings were at: http://natmus.dk/en/historical-knowledge/denmark/prehistoric-period-until-1050-ad/the-viking-age/

The Vikings were from the areas that are now Denmark, Norway and Sweden. In the few hundred years before the Viking Age, sometimes called the Vendel era, the **Germanic** peoples of Scandinavia had grown rich through trade in iron, fur and slaves. They lived in groups called **clans**, ruled by chiefs. They told stories of brave heroes who, just like their own clan chiefs, rode into battle on horseback and wore fine armour.

As the people prospered and the population grew, it became difficult for farmers to produce enough food. There was rich soil along coasts and river valleys, but inland Scandinavia was made up of woods, heaths and rocky mountains. Around 750 CE, the Vikings began to raid nearby lands, snatching treasures and slaves. Their name may come from *vikingr*, an Old **Norse** word meaning 'pirate' or 'raider'. Old Norse was the language of the Vikings.

This seventh-century helmet dates to the Vendel era, just before the Viking Age. It was found at Uppland in Sweden.

Viking raiders travelled in longships with prows carved to look like scary beasts.

Not everyone described the Vikings as wild barbarians. In 1220 the English historian John of Wallingford wrote:

'[T]hey were – according to their country's customs – in the habit of combing their hair every day, to bathe every Saturday, to change their clothes frequently...'

Their raids gained the Vikings a reputation as ruthless warriors. However, most people stayed at home, working the land or making a living by crafting goods in metal, leather or wood. Some were shrewd traders. There were shipbuilders, who specialized in constructing elegant **longships**. Vikings established peaceful settlements in other lands, including Greenland and Iceland. Wherever they were, Vikings told imaginative and exciting stories called **sagas**. They worshipped the same gods and goddesses and believed in an afterlife. They thought that dead heroes went to **Valhalla**, a great hall where there was feasting each evening. They buried their dead with **grave goods** and sometimes commemorated them with engraved stones called **runestones**.

This stone shows the Norse god Odin arriving at Valhalla on his eight-legged horse, Sleipnir.

🐾 **What two forms of transport appear on the picture stone?**

WHY DID THE VIKINGS TRAVEL SO MUCH?

The Vikings lived mainly along the coasts of Scandinavia and in fertile regions in the south. In the north, no one ventured far inland because the terrain was rough and the climate bitterly cold for much of the year. Travel was usually by sea to other lands. The Vikings who took to the sea were traders, raiders or explorers.

Viking merchants sailed far and wide buying and selling goods. From Scandinavia they brought timber, iron and furs. Viking territories were also a source of whale and seal skins for making ropes, whale bones and walrus tusks for carving, and amber for jewellery. Traders transported these goods east across the Baltic Sea and then overland to Russia, or around northwestern Europe and into the Mediterranean. They returned with wheat, honey, wool and tin from Britain; wine, salt, pottery and gold from southern Europe; and glass, spices, silks and silver from the east.

From their homelands, the Vikings sailed west over the Atlantic, east across the Baltic and south as far as the Mediterranean.

These silver coins were probably minted at Hedeby, Denmark in the early 800s. They show Viking merchant ships.

DETECTIVE WORK

Explore a clickable map that reveals where the Vikings travelled: http://www.pbs.org/wgbh/nova/vikings/diaspora.html

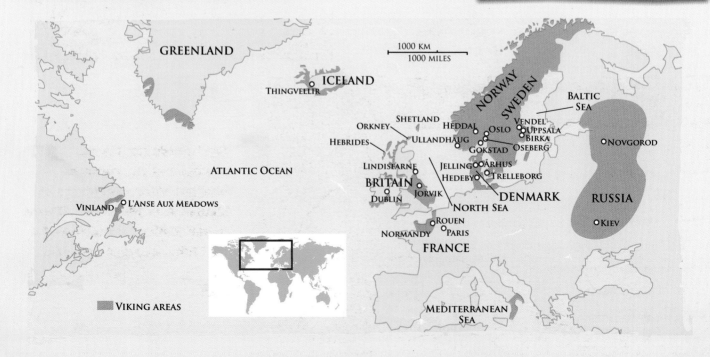

GREENLAND

1000 KM
1000 MILES

ICELAND
THINGVELLIR

NORWAY
SWEDEN
BALTIC SEA

ORKNEY
SHETLAND
HEDDAL
OSLO
VENDEL
UPPSALA
BIRKA
HEBRIDES
ULLANDHAUG
GOKSTAD
OSEBERG
NOVGOROD

LINDISFARNE
JELLING
ÅRHUS
BRITAIN
HEDEBY
TRELLEBORG
JORVIK
DUBLIN
DENMARK
RUSSIA
NORTH SEA
KIEV

ATLANTIC OCEAN

VINLAND
L'ANSE AUX MEADOWS

ROUEN
NORMANDY
PARIS
FRANCE

MEDITERRANEAN SEA

▮ VIKING AREAS

Some Vikings found an easier way to bring back booty – by terrorizing western Europe, plundering its treasures and taking the people they didn't kill as slaves. The first dated raid was on the monastery at Lindisfarne, England on 8 June, 793. Vikings initially targeted the North Sea and English Channel coasts, but before long they were sailing inland. In 845 they even took Paris, forcing the French king to pay a **ransom**. Sometimes the Vikings swooped in, took everything of value and then left, torching the place as they went. Occasionally, they settled near where they landed, setting up a base from which to attack other targets.

Vikings also travelled in order to find new places to live. These daring explorers discovered the Faroe Islands, Iceland and distant Greenland, where Erik the Red founded a settlement. His son, Leif Ericsson, ventured further across the Atlantic and established a colony at 'Vinland', a site that was probably L'Anse Aux Meadows, Newfoundland, in modern-day Canada. Vikings settled in northern Scotland, too, on Orkney and Shetland.

The *Saga of the Greenlanders* tells how Vikings discovered Vinland in North America:

'The nature of the country was, as they thought, so good that cattle would not require house feeding in winter, for there came no frost in winter, and little did the grass wither there. Day and night were more equal than in Greenland or Iceland.'

In this sixteenth-century woodcut, Viking raiders carry a weapon-laden boat into Russia.

🐾 **What weapons are inside the boat that the Vikings are carrying?**

Archaeologists have discovered the remains of eight Viking buildings at L'Anse Aux Meadows. There is now a reconstruction of a turf longhouse at the site.

WHO WERE THE VIKING LEADERS?

Before the Viking Age, each clan had its own chief. Then, between the ninth and tenth centuries stronger rulers appeared, who conquered rival chieftains and created united kingdoms in Denmark, Norway and Sweden. The rest of society was made up of nobles (*jarls*), freemen (*karls*) and slaves (*thralls*).

The early chiefs were the leaders of their clans but they were not all-powerful. They had to obey the rulings of the local assembly, which was called a **Thing**. Every district had its own Thing, which met yearly and where every free person could say what they thought and talk through their disagreements, though only men could vote. At the start of a Thing, the region's laws were read out as a reminder to everyone. Small disputes carried on being sorted out at Things even after the Vikings had kings.

DETECTIVE WORK

Investigate the tax that Anglo-Saxons in England had to pay to their overlords, the Danish kings: http://primaryfacts. com/3148/danegeld-facts- and-information/

One Viking state, Iceland, never had kings. It held ordinary Things to decide matters of law at a local level, and there was also a national assembly called the Althing, which met at Thingvellir for a fortnight each summer. As well as being a parliament, the Althing was a massive trading post and festival.

Denmark was probably united under one ruler in the ninth century, but there is not much information about its early kings. The first about whom we know much was Harald Bluetooth, who ruled from 958 to 987. His kingdom stretched into southern Norway and he built forts to keep control of his territory (see page 11).

Thingvellir is 44 km east of Reykjavik, the capital of modern-day Iceland. From 930 it was the site of the Viking parliament, or Althing.

This fresco shows Olaf II of Norway (r. 1015-28). He teamed up with Sweden to wage war on Cnut, but was defeated and sent into exile.

What's behind King Olaf's crown on the fresco?

Harald Bluetooth was overthrown by his son Sweyn Forkbeard (r. 986-1014), who conquered England, making it part of the Danish Empire. Sweyn's son Cnut (r. 1016-35) was the most powerful Danish king of all, adding some of Sweden to the lands he controlled.

Norway's first king was the popular Harald Fairhair (r. 872-930). After his death there was unrest as his sons squabbled for power. Key Swedish kings included Eric the Victorious (r. 975-95) and his son Olof Skötkonung (r. 995-1022), who tried to **convert** Sweden to Christianity (see page 26).

The might of King Cnut and his fleet was described in an eleventh-century Norman manuscript called the *Encomium Emmae Reginae*:

'For who could look upon... the men of metal, menacing with golden face... upon the bulls on the ships threatening death, their horns shining with gold, without feeling any fear for the king of such a force? Furthermore, in this great expedition there was present no slave... all were noble, all strong with the might of mature age, all sufficiently fit for any type of fighting...'

King Olof Skötkonung of Sweden was a Christian, but most of his subjects still worshipped the Norse gods.

WHY WERE THE VIKINGS GOOD AT FIGHTING?

Being brave and fearless was part of Viking culture. Boys grew up listening to tales of heroic warriors and learned to handle weapons from an early age. As adults, they were expected to volunteer to join their chief or king's army in times of conflict. A few became professional soldiers, paid to protect leaders or guard cargo ships.

Viking weapons were legendary. **Bladesmiths** made swords by heating iron rods, twisting them together and then hammering them flat – the resulting weapons were strong, flexible and double-edged for slashing. Swords were costly, so if they were damaged in battle they were mended. Warriors were sometimes buried with these prized possessions, but more often they handed them down to their sons. Swords were even given names! King Magnus Barefoot of Norway called his 'Legbiter'. Spears were a common weapon and there were two kinds – a light javelin for throwing, and a longer spear for use in hand-to-hand combat. Battleaxes were about a metre long, with a rounded blade. Some men carried bows and arrows.

The Vikings in this medieval illustration are armed with iron-tipped spears, ready to land on the French coast.

The tenth-century Arab chronicler Ahmad ibn Fadlan described the Viking merchants he met on his travels:

'Each man has an axe, a sword and a knife and keeps each by him at all times. The swords are broad and grooved, of Frankish sort. Every man is tattooed from fingernails to neck with dark green (or green or blue-black) trees, figures, etc.'

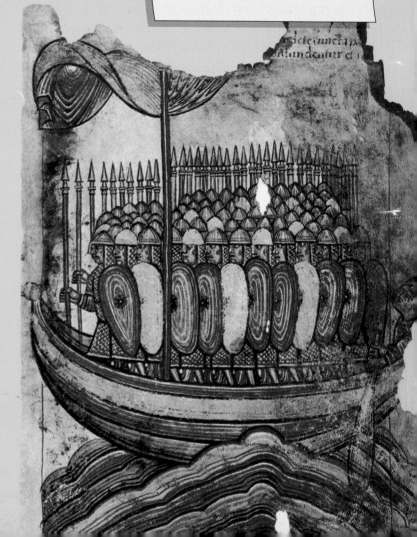

DETECTIVE WORK

Find out about warriors' weapons: http://jorvik-viking-centre.co.uk/wp-content/uploads/2012/10/Weapons.pdf

The fighters who could afford the best armour were nobles and professional soldiers. They protected their upper body with a chainmail tunic called a *byrnie*, while poorer fighters made do with a padded leather jacket. Viking helmets were made of metal or leather. Warriors carried a wooden shield, sometimes reinforced with leather, with a metal cap in the centre that protected their hand. Early ones were round but later in the Viking Age kite-shaped shields were made.

Fighting forces were usually assembled at the start of summer, which was the raiding season. In times of conflict, however, rulers needed troops all year round. In the 1930s, **archaeologists** found the remains of a circular fort at Trelleborg in Denmark. Since then, four more ring forts have been discovered. They probably date to the reign of Harald Bluetooth, who needed to make sure there were no uprisings in the surrounding areas. The fort at Trelleborg housed 1,300 soldiers.

This silver pendant shows a typical Viking helmet of the early 900s.

Did Vikings wear horned helmets?

Sixteen longhouses served as barracks at Trelleborg. One has been reconstructed.

WHAT WERE VIKING FARMS LIKE?

Most Vikings were farmers. Everyone in the family helped to tend the crops and look after the animals. A small number of wealthy farmers paid for help with skilled tasks, and owned slaves to carry out the physical work.

At the centre of the farm was the **longhouse**, where everyone lived and slept. There were sheds to shelter the animals in winter and storehouses for keeping food and wood. Most farms were self-sufficient. They were sited next to a stream, river or lake that provided fresh water, and the people aimed to produce enough food for themselves, with perhaps some extra to sell. Rather than buy tools, the farm had its own **forge** where iron could be smelted. Farmers also produced their own cloth from flax and wool, and **tanned** their own leather.

A Norwegian trader called Ottar described the geography of Norway to King Alfred of Wessex:

'All that they can either graze or plough lies by the sea, and even that is very rocky in some places; and to the east, and alongside the cultivated land, lie wild mountains.'

DETECTIVE WORK

Look around a reconstructed Viking farm here: http://www.youtube.com/watch?v=nEkSWmTekI0

Farm buildings had stone walls and turf roofs. This is a reconstruction at the Viking farm at Ullandhaug, near Stavangar in Norway.

Viking farms were mixed – there were animals and crops. Livestock included sheep, cows, goats, pigs, horses, poultry and geese. Milk from the sheep, cows and goats was drunk or turned into butter and cheese. Animals provided meat and eggs, leather, wool and feathers for bedding. Only the hardiest animals survived the harsh Scandinavian winters. In the far north, people farmed reindeer for their milk, meat and hides.

Each spring, farmers used a simple plough called an *ard* to break up the ground, then planted cereal crops, such as spelt, barley, oats and rye. They fertilized the soil with animal dung and kept it free of weeds with a metal hoe. In late summer, the grain was harvested using sickles. It was ground into flour between **quern stones**. People set aside plots for growing vegetables. In winter, the men went off hunting to find additional food for the pot.

Sheep provided wool, milk and meat. The hardy Hebridean sheep farmed by Vikings in the Hebrides could survive in areas with sparse vegetation.

Spelt, an early form of wheat, was one of the main cereal crops.

What did Vikings use to grind grain?

WHAT WERE VIKING TOWNS LIKE?

Most Viking settlements were farming communities, but there were a few large towns. Hedeby in Denmark, Birka in Sweden, Jorvik (York) in England and Dublin in Ireland were the busiest ports and trading posts. As well as merchants, they drew in specialist tradesmen and craftworkers.

Viking towns were crowded, smoky, smelly and noisy. Dealers came to buy and sell goods including slaves, furs and walrus ivory. There were also local market traders – fishermen selling their catch of the day; ironworkers producing swords and other weapons; and market gardeners displaying their vegetables for sale. Craftsmen built the longships that chiefs used for their summer raiding parties.

DETECTIVE WORK

Read about Århus, a Viking town in Denmark: http://www.vikingeskibsmuseet.dk/en/the-sea-stallion-past-and-present/the-viking-age-in-scandinavia/aarhus/#.Uqt24qWaKf0

These buildings and log street are part of a reconstruction of Hedeby, the largest Danish port.

Towns were crammed with buildings and animal enclosures. Some houses were built from wooden planks, produced by splitting tree trunks, while others were made of **wattle and daub**. Roofs were thatched with straw or reeds, so they often caught fire.

The tenth-century Arab traveller Ibrahim ibn Yaqub al-Tartushi visited Hedeby and wrote:

'Slesvig (Hedeby) is a very large town at the extreme end of the world ocean... People eat mainly fish which exist in abundance.'

What were Viking streets made of?

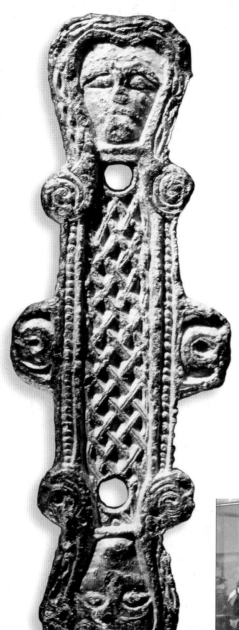

Most of the buildings nearest the port belonged to craftsmen. Here, tanners produced leather goods, coopers made storage barrels and smiths worked with iron. Other workers specialized in carving wood or crafting jewellery. If they were rich, they lived elsewhere with their families, but poorer workers slept in a corner of their workshops.

Along the quay, huge warehouses stored imports and exports, while shipbuilders made and repaired ships in their yards. Cargo vessels docked in the harbour long enough for their owners to trade their wares at a profit and pick up new things to sell abroad. Wooden wagons pulled by oxen or horses trundled down the streets transporting goods. The roads were made from logs so they were extremely bumpy, and slippery when wet. Ordinary people got around on foot, while wealthier folk rode horses. In winter, when the ground was frozen, people used sleighs, sledges and skis.

This gilt copper bridle bit was probably made by a craftsman in Viking Dublin.

Everyday carts would not have been so intricately carved as this one. It was part of a ship burial for a very important Viking.

WHAT WAS IT LIKE ON BOARD A VIKING BOAT?

The Vikings were brilliant shipbuilders. They are famous for the slender, seagoing warships with carved prows that they used for raids, but they also built other kinds of craft. There were large and small cargo ships called *knarrs* and *karves*, as well as fishing boats and canoes.

Viking raiders carried out their attacks in spring and summer, when the seas were calmest. Their longships were light enough to pick up and carry if necessary, and narrow enough to sail up rivers for surprise inland strikes. They had a sail, possibly made of wool, and oars – between twenty-four and fifty, depending on the size of the ship. Some carried as few as twelve men, while the largest transported up to one hundred and twenty, with room for horses too. The Vikings gave their vessels names such as *The Long Serpent* or *Wind Raven*. On long voyages, the men rowed in shifts, sitting on sea chests that contained their few belongings. The lookout stood in the stern, near the steersman. At night the men came ashore if they could. If they were too far from land, they slept on board in sealskin sleeping bags, with the sail pulled down over them for shelter. They ate bread and sun-dried fish and drank water or beer.

Gareth Williams of the British Museum described *Roskilde 6*, which carried up to a hundred warriors:

'This ship was a troop carrier. There are records in the annals of fleets of hundreds of ships, so you could be talking about an army of up to 10,000 men suddenly landing on your coast, highly trained, fit, capable of moving very fast on water or land.'

The longship's square sail was probably made of wool, criss-crossed with strips of leather that helped keep its shape.

DETECTIVE WORK
Watch video clips of a reconstructed Viking longboat: http://www. vikingeskibsmuseet.dk/ en/about-us/news-room/ movie-clips/sea-stallion/#. Uqt2L6WaKf0

The Vikings carved the prows of their longships to look like fearsome beasts. Ones with a dragon were nicknamed 'dragon ships'.

*Knarr*s were wider, deeper and slower than longships. They carried thirty to forty people. The middle of the boat had a large, open area that could be packed with goods or even livestock. Sailors did not have navigational instruments. They steered by the sun and stars or looked out for landmarks described to them by other seafarers. They also observed sea birds and fish shoals to work out how near they were to shore.

Boats were central to Viking death as well as life. Dead noblemen or women were placed in them along with their prized possessions, vehicles such as carts and sleighs, and sometimes servants, horses, dogs or hunting birds. Early in the Viking Age, these craft were launched out to sea and set alight. Later, they were buried under earth mounds. The most famous **ship burials** are at Gokstad and Oseberg in southern Norway.

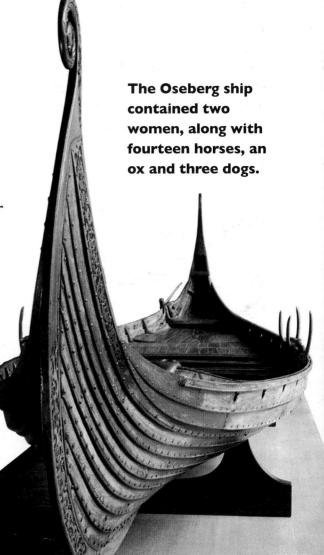

The Oseberg ship contained two women, along with fourteen horses, an ox and three dogs.

🐾 **Did the planks that made up the hulls of Viking boats overlap or not?**

WHAT DID THE VIKINGS EAT AND DRINK?

Most Viking settlements were along coasts or up rivers, so the people consumed a lot of fish. They also ate the meat, grains and dairy products from their farms. Porridge was a staple food, made by mixing spelt, oats or barley with milk or water. People ate barley bread or, if they were wealthy, wheat bread. Grinding the grain was tiring work.

DETECTIVE WORK

Click on Videos to watch a film about Viking food: www.bbc.co.uk/schools/primaryhistory/vikings/vikings_at_home/

The Vikings ate a wide variety of different fish. Catches included herring, cod, haddock, salmon, trout and eel. They ate shellfish, such as mussels. During the winter, rivers froze over and seas were too rough to sail in, so people ate preserved fish that had been smoked, dried or pickled in salt water. Meat could be kept by these methods, too. Slaves harvested salt by boiling seawater so that the water evaporated leaving the salt behind.

People hunted whales, seals and walruses. In winter, they tracked animals on land, killing deer, wild boar, elk, bears, foxes, otters and rabbits. They used spears, bows and arrows or traps. They shot ducks, gulls and other wild birds with their arrows, and collected their eggs. They caught great auks, too, which were flightless birds related to puffins. They usually saved their own livestock for special feast days, but each autumn they slaughtered any beasts that looked too weak to last the winter.

The Vikings preserved fish for winter by hanging it out to dry in the wind or sun.

The Vikings grew cabbages, peas, beans, carrots and turnips in their vegetable gardens, and collected berries, nuts and edible flowers from the wild. They cooked stews in huge cauldrons that hung over the hearth and spit-roasted meat and fish over the fire. The food was flavoured with wild herbs, garlic, onions and leeks, as well as spices such as cumin from the east. The meal was washed down with ale brewed from barley and hops, mead made from honey, or milk. The milk was warmed in a pig's-bladder bag by dropping in hot stones. Rich people sometimes drank wine fermented from grapes imported from southern Europe. The poor used simple, wooden mugs but nobles had fancy **drinking horns**.

What was the main ingredient in mead?

Viking cauldrons were made of iron or soapstone. They were suspended from a tripod or hung from a chain over the roof beam.

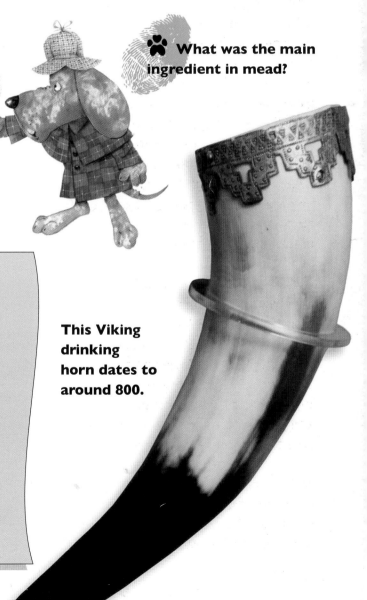

This Viking drinking horn dates to around 800.

Archaeologists Graham and Merryn Dineley have researched how and where Vikings brewed beer:

'*We know that the Vikings drank ale. There are numerous references to it in the sagas. We also know that the ale was made from malt. In the tenth century… Haakon Haroldson, the first Christian king of Norway, decreed that Yule be celebrated on Christmas Day and that every farmstead "should brew two meals of malt into ale". One brew was for family, the other for guests. There were fines for [not obeying]. If they failed to brew for three years in a row their farm was [taken from them].*'

WHAT DID VIKINGS DO FOR FUN?

Eating and drinking was one of the chief pleasures for the Vikings – even their idea of heaven was a feast hall! The Vikings believed that dead heroes went to Valhalla, where there was always plenty of boar stew, mead and ale. The Vikings also loved listening to stories and playing games or sports.

Vikings did not have a lot of leisure time. For women, most of the day was taken up with preparing food, spinning and weaving and looking after their children. Farmers had to tend to crops and livestock. Warriors practised their fighting techniques and repaired broken weapons. If there was any free time during the day, the Vikings enjoyed outdoor activities, such as swimming, fishing and boating. In winter they had fun skiing, sledging and skating.

After the evening meal, people told stories. The Norse sagas that were eventually written down in Iceland in the thirteenth and fourteenth centuries are based on tales that had been handed down **orally** for many generations. They mix history with folklore, telling of Viking heroes and adventurers, explorations and voyages, feuds and family chronicles. A favourite one was about the hero Sigurd slaying the dragon, Fáfnir. Sometimes there was music to accompany the sagas or poems, or just to listen to on its own. People played recorders and panpipes carved from wood or bone, or blew into horns from cows or goats. There were stringed instruments such as harps and lyres. The Vikings did not have a way of writing music down, though, so no one can be sure what it sounded like.

Ibrahim Ibn Ahmad Al-Tartushi, an Arab merchant, visited Denmark around 950 and wrote:

'Never before have I heard uglier songs than those of the Vikings… The growling sound coming from their throats reminds me of dogs howling, only more untamed.'

In this carving, Prince Gunnar is dying in a snake pit, playing the harp with his toes. Gunnar was a character in the saga of Sigurd.

The Vikings played board games – a popular one was *hneftafl*, a chess-like game of strategy. One player had eight pieces, which he or she used to guard the king from their opponent, who had sixteen pieces. Some sets were beautifully carved from wood, walrus ivory or amber, but Vikings also scratched out boards on the ground and played with scraps of bone or shards of broken pottery.

DETECTIVE WORK

Listen to some Viking sagas here: www. bbc.co.uk/learning/ schoolradio/subjects/ english/viking_sagas

What were the Lewis chessmen carved from?

▲ This rook is part of a Viking chess set found on the Isle of Lewis. It is carved from walrus ivory.

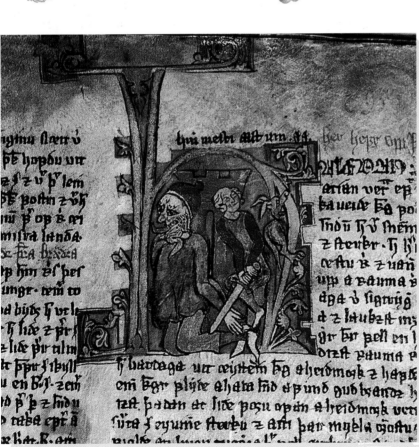

◄ This is part of an Icelandic manuscript containing many of the Norse sagas. It shows King Harald Fairhair freeing a giant.

WHO WERE THE VIKING GODS?

The Vikings believed in numerous gods and goddesses (deities), and told legends about them and other supernatural beings. Their myths included a story that explained how the world was created, and another that predicted its destruction. The Vikings called the end of the world *Ragnarök*, a word meaning 'doom of the gods'.

The main Viking deities were Odin, Thor, Frey and Freya. One-eyed Odin was the god of wisdom, war and poetry. He was said to have given people the gift of writing with **runes** (see page 24). Thor looked after law and order, and carried a magic hammer called Mjölnir. When they heard thunder, people said it was the rumbling wheels of Thor's chariot. Frey was the god of fertility and birth. His twin sister, Freya, was the goddess of love and death and could tell the future. Her chariot was pulled across the sky by cats. Loki was a trickster figure. In some stories he was a god, while in others he was a giant. He was responsible for killing Odin's favourite son, Balder, and for plotting to bring about the end of the world.

In the *Prose Edda*, a character called Third says who the main Viking god is:

'Odin is the highest and oldest of the gods. He rules in all matters, and, although the other gods are powerful, all serve him as children do their father. Frigg is his wife. She knows the fates of men, even though she pronounces no prophecies.'

🐾 **What was the name of Thor's hammer?**

This pendant shows the goddess Freya. She is wearing a precious necklace that was given to her by four dwarves.

The Vikings believed that Odin and his brothers Vili and Ve had created the universe, and had also made the first man, Ask, and woman, Embla. An enormous ash tree called Yggdrasil held the universe together and connected its nine worlds, each of which was inhabited by a different kind of being. Humans lived in Midgard, for example, while the sky and earth gods lived in Asgard and Vanaheim. Dead heroes travelled from Midgard to Asgard along a rainbow bridge to reach Valhalla. Other worlds belonged to giants, elves, dwarves and the dead. Two – ice-covered Niflheim and fiery Muspelheim – had existed since before creation.

Vikings worshipped their gods outdoors, in temples and at small shrines in their own homes. They made sacrifices to them, killing animals and hanging them up on trees or throwing jewels and weapons into bogs or rivers. People prayed to the gods for protection and wore protective charms called amulets to keep them safe.

▶ **Odin was said to have given an eye in return for knowledge. On this statue, the god's left eye is open and seeing but the right is closed shut.**

This brooch represents one of Loki's children, a sea serpent that encircles the human world, Midgard.

DETECTIVE WORK

Watch an animation explaining how Vikings thought the world was created: www.bigmyth. com/myths/english/2_ norse_full.htm

WHAT ART DID THE VIKINGS MAKE?

The Vikings created beautiful carvings in wood and also on stones. There are image stones with pictures on them and runestones that have written inscriptions. Skilful Viking metalworkers made exquisite treasures in gold, silver and gilded bronze. The stories and myths that Vikings left behind are a form of art, too.

DETECTIVE WORK

Find out about runes and runic inscriptions: runic-dictionary.nottingham.ac.uk

The well-preserved wooden objects that have been found in ship burials are wonderfully carved, though it is unlikely that everyday items were as intricate. People were buried with their best belongings for the afterlife, including wagons and sledges, ships' prows and storage chests.

People placed magnificent memorial stones by the side of the road where passers-by could admire them. The stones commemorated gods and heroes or dead relatives. The writing on them was in symbols called runes, which were easy to carve because they were made up of straight or diagonal lines. The runic alphabet used during the Viking Age is known as the younger futhark. It had developed from an earlier alphabet in use before 750 that is called the elder futhark. The younger one was made up of sixteen symbols and there were two versions: long-branch runes and short-twig runes. After a runestone had been inscribed, it was painted to make it more eye-catching. Popular colours included red, white and black. Paints were made by mixing **pigments** with fat and water.

🐾 **What does gilded mean?**

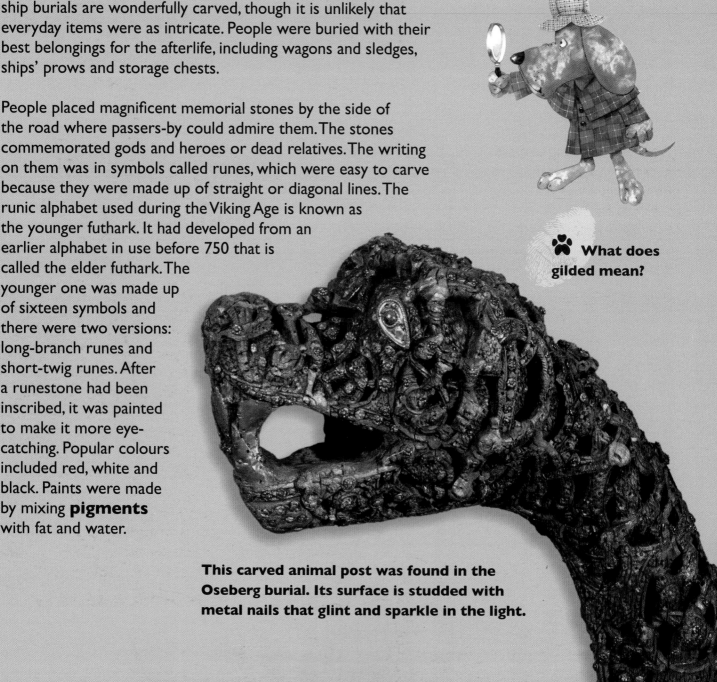

This carved animal post was found in the Oseberg burial. Its surface is studded with metal nails that glint and sparkle in the light.

Viking metalworkers created delicate brooches, cloak pins, arm rings, pendants and even bridle bits for horses. They liked very detailed organic patterns of interwoven shapes and lines or representations of animals. The very rich could afford gold or silver. Cheaper metals, such as copper and bronze, were sometimes **gilded** to make them look like gold.

Long-branch runes (top row) were probably used for inscriptions. The simpler short-twig runes (bottom row) may have been for everyday writing.

ᚠᚢᚦᛅᚱᛈ ᚼᚾᛁᛏᛋ ᛏᛒᛦᛚᛘ

ᚠᚼᚦᛅᚱᛈ ᚼᛏᛁᛆ' ᛌᛂᛏᛏᛁ

fuþąrk hnias tbmlʀ

The runes snaking around this stone say it was put up in memory of a man called Jóarr or Ívarr.

Fabulous brooches, like this one made of gold, were given as gifts and worn as status symbols.

Archaeologist Ole Thirup Kastholm of the Roskilde Museum describes the discovery of a spectacular brooch at a farm on Zealand:

'The decoration consists of a central wheel cross in relief, with inlaid gold pressed into a waffle form. The waffle gold is in some areas covered with transparent red glass or semi-precious stones and forming an equal-armed cross.'

WHAT HAPPENED TO THE VIKINGS?

The Viking Age came to an end after people in Scandinavia converted to Christianity and stopped their violent raids. The last attack on England took place in 1153 and the final one on Scotland was in 1263. Although the traditional Viking way of life died out, the people lived on as Christian Danes, Swedes and Norwegians.

Viking raiders and merchants encountered Christianity on their travels, but soon missionaries were arriving in Scandinavia from mainland Europe. Harald Bluetooth was the first Danish king to become a Christian and he boasted on a runestone at Jelling that he had made all his subjects Christian, too. The Norwegians adopted the faith in the early eleventh century, during the reigns of Olaf Tryggvason (r. 995-1000) and Olaf II Haraldsson (r. 1015-28). Sweden officially became Christian in 1008, when King Olof Skötkonung (r. 995-1022) was baptized. Once they were Christian, the people of Scandinavia no longer worshipped the Norse gods and goddesses.

▲ Scandinavian peoples built beautiful wooden churches. This one in Heddal, Norway, dates to the early 1200s.

◀ This stone at Jelling was erected by Harald Bluetooth of Denmark. It is three-sided. This side shows Christ on the cross.

English historians sometimes give the year 1066 as an end date for the Viking Age. That year saw two invasions of England – the first was by Vikings from Norway, led by Harald Hardrada. He is known as the 'last Viking' and he died at Stamford Bridge fighting the Anglo-Saxon king of England, Harold Godwinsson. Soon after, Harold Godwinsson was defeated at Hastings by William, Duke of Normandy. William himself was a descendant of the Vikings – Normandy is named after the Norse men who settled there. William went on to conquer all of England. In Scotland, Vikings remained lords of the isles until the 1200s.

Harald Hardrada, who attempted to invade England in 1066, was a ruthless king. He said:

'Treason must be stopped by fair means or foul.'

DETECTIVE WORK

Discover the Bayeux Tapestry, which commemorates events in England in 1066, including the defeat of Harold Godwinsson by William: www.tapestry-bayeux.com

Although the Viking way of life died out, its influence continued. Norse stories and sagas have thrilled listeners through the centuries. The remains of Viking houses, burials and treasure hoards can be seen in museums, giving a glimpse of what their culture was like. More than six thousand runestones still stand, and the Viking language also lives on in the names of places and days of the week. Swansea, for example, comes from the Norse words meaning 'Sveinn's Place', while Scarborough means 'Scarth's Town'.

Which day of the week takes its name from the Norse god Thor?

This twelfth-century Swedish tapestry shows Christians ringing the bells of their church in order to scare off evil spirits and the old Viking gods.

YOUR PROJECT

By now you should have collected lots of information about the Vikings and their interesting history. This is the time to consider what sort of project you might like to produce.

You could make your own model longship. Have a look in museums, books or on websites for real ones to copy. Another idea would be to research Viking kings and draw their family trees. Some of their names are very colourful. You might prefer to create a timeline showing the history of the Vikings in Britain – when they carried out their raids and where they settled.

If you are interested in Viking language, look back at the rune symbols on page 25 and the sounds they represent. Can you write your name in runes? Do not worry if some of the letters you need are missing. Just use those for which there are runes. Look at a map of Britain and search for evidence of Viking names. They include ones that end with -by (which meant farm or village), -gate (road) or -kirk (church).

You might have your own ideas for a project, but whatever you decide, remember it is your project, so choose something that interests you. Good luck!

Stories of Viking rulers mix fact and fiction. Sweyn Forkbeard died of natural causes, but this illustration from the 1300s shows Saint Edmund killing him.

Look in your local museum for Viking artefacts, like these beautifully preserved leather shoes.

Project presentation

● Do plenty of research before you begin. Use the Internet and your local and/or school library. Is there a nearby museum or historical site related to your project? Scan the television guide for programmes about Vikings.

● If you were a news reporter and could travel back in time, what questions would you ask the Vikings? Make a list, and then see if you can answer them yourself through your research.

Find examples of Viking art or craftsmanship. This mould was used to make plaques to decorate warriors' helmets.

GLOSSARY

archaeologist Someone who studies the remains of past societies.

bladesmith Someone who specializes in making knives and swords.

CE 'Common Era'. Used to signify years since the believed birth of Jesus.

clan A group of close-knit and interrelated families.

convert To persuade someone to adopt a different religion or set of beliefs.

drinking horn A drinking vessel made from a cow's hollow, curved horn.

exile Banishment from one's own land.

forge A place where metal artefacts are made by heating and hammering.

freeman Someone who is not a slave.

Germanic Describes prehistoric peoples originating from northern and western Europe.

gilded Covered thinly with gold.

grave goods Objects placed with a dead body for use in the afterlife.

longhouse A large, rectangular dwelling made of wood, stone or earth and turf.

longship A Viking warship, powered by lines of rowers and a single, rectangular sail.

Norse From Scandinavia, especially Norway.

orally Not written down, but passed on by word of mouth.

pigment A substance used to give colouring. Ochre from the earth, for example, is a reddish-brown pigment.

quern stone A flat, circular stone used as part of a pair for grinding grain into flour.

ransom Money paid to secure the release of a person or even a whole city.

rune A 'letter' from the Viking alphabet.

runestone A memorial stone carved with writing and pictures.

saga A long story that tells of heroic adventures.

ship burial A grave where a dead person's body is placed inside a ship with possessions for the afterlife, and then buried under a mound of earth.

supernatural Something that is hard to explain using the ordinary laws of nature.

tan To turn animal skin into leather.

Thing A local assembly where every freeman could say what they thought.

tripod A three-legged stand or support.

Valhalla The god Odin's banqueting hall in Asgard, the realm of the gods, where heroes went when they died.

wattle and daub Built of posts and twigs (wattle) and clay or mud and straw (daub).

ANSWERS

Page 5   A longboat and a horse appear on the runestone.
Page 6   The boat contains bows and arrows and axes.
Page 9   There is a halo behind Olaf's crown. After his death he was made a saint for his role in converting Norway to Christianity.
Page 10   There is no evidence that Vikings wore horned helmets, but they appear in them in popular culture in paintings, cartoons and movies.
Page 13   The Vikings used round, flat stones called quern stones to grind grain.
Page 14   The Vikings built their streets from logs.
Page 17   The planks overlapped. Hulls built like this are described as clinker-built.
Page 18   Mead is made from honey.
Page 20   There are nearly eighty Lewis chessmen. Most are made of walrus ivory (tusks) but some are carved from whales' teeth.
Page 23   Thor's hammer was called Mjölnir.
Page 25   Gilded means being given a thin coating of gold.
Page 27   Thursday is named after the Viking god Thor.

FURTHER INFORMATION

Books to read

Viking (Eyewitness) by Susan M. Margeson (Dorling Kindersley, 2011)
The Viking Codex: The Saga of Leif Eriksson by Fiona Macdonald (Book House, 2011)
Viking World by Philippa Wingate and Anne Millard (Usborne, 2008)
Vikings (100 Facts) by Fiona Macdonald (Miles Kelly, 2008)

Websites

http://www.bbc.co.uk/schools/primaryhistory/vikings/
http://www.ngkids.co.uk/did-you-know/10_facts_about_the_vikings
http://www.primaryhomeworkhelp.co.uk/vikings.html

Note to parents and teachers: Every effort has been made by the publishers to ensure that these websites are suitable for children. However, because of the nature of the Internet, it is impossible to guarantee that the contents of these sites will not be altered. We strongly advise that Internet access is supervised by a responsible adult.

Places to visit

British Museum, London WC1B 3DG
Jorvik Viking Centre, York YO1 9WT
National Museum of Scotland, Edinburgh EH1 1JF
Up Helly Aa festival, Lerwick, Shetland Islands

INDEX

Numbers in **bold** refer to pictures and captions